THE BLACK STUDENT PLAYBOOK
Strategies for Succeeding at a PWI

J. McCarthy, PhD, MBA

The Black Student Playbook:
Strategies for Succeeding at a PWI

Copyright © 2025 by J. McCarthy
All rights reserved.

No part of this publication may be copied, stored, transmitted, or reproduced in any form or by any means—electronic, mechanical, photocopying, recording, or otherwise—without the prior written permission of the publisher, except in the case of brief quotations used in reviews, articles, or scholarly works.

For permissions, inquiries, or bulk orders, please contact:
rlspublishing@gmail.com

This book is intended for informational and inspirational purposes only. It is not a substitute for professional advice. The author and publisher make no guarantees regarding the results that individuals may experience from the information provided.

Published by The Real Life Series Publishing Co., LLC
www.thereallifeseries.com

Printed in the United States of America
First Edition, June 2025

ISBN: 979-8-9989754-1-7
Library of Congress Control Number: 2025910948

DEDICATION

This is dedicated to my late mother, Linda J. McCarthy, who deferred her own dreams of education so that mine could take flight. Her sacrifice became my foundation, her love my guiding light. I attempt to carry her legacy of youth mentorship, hoping to impact even a fraction of the lives she touched.

TABLE OF CONTENTS

Laying The Foundation

Preface | 1
Roots | 5
Awakening | 11
Setting the Stage | 17

The 10 Lessons

Lesson I - Hygiene & First Impressions | 25
Lesson II - Cultivating Identity & Spirituality | 35
Lesson III - Building Relationships | 45
Lesson IV - Navigating Networks & Black Spaces | 55
Lesson V - Academic Discipline | 63
Lesson VI - Healthy Living | 77
Lesson VII - Resources & Support | 85
Lesson VIII - Staying Safe | 93
Lesson IX - Handling Adversity | 101
Lesson X - Seizing Opportunities | 109

Moving Forward

Closing Comments | 117

Reference Materials

Appendix A: Resource Directory | 123
Appendix B: Cultivating Identity & Spirituality | 131
Appendix C: Additional Reading & Resources | 135

About The Author | 139
Other RLS Titles | 140

"Starin' Through My Rear View"
Preface

PREFACE

Before diving into advice and strategies, I want to share my journey with you. This isn't just about establishing credibility; it's about showing you that finishing strong is possible regardless of where you start. I grew up in the inner city with limited resources, went to college as a first-generation student, and often felt out of place in spaces that were not built with me in mind. Those experiences shaped the lessons I'm about to share.

The next few pages aren't just my story; they might be your story too. Or perhaps your parents' story. Or maybe your background is entirely different, and you were raised in a dual-parent household in a middle-class suburban community.

Regardless of where you began, the ten core lessons I will share are rooted in truths I learned through both success and struggle, transcending individual circumstances while honoring our shared experiences. You are not alone on this journey.

In this book, you'll find real talk, relatable stories, and the unfiltered advice I wish someone had given me before I stepped onto campus. The goal is simple: to help you move smart. That means learning how to manage your time, protect your peace, build the right network, and keep your eyes on the bigger picture. Every lesson in this playbook is designed to help you do just that: move smart and move with purpose.

Now, you might notice something unique about the chapter pages as you read. The song references that appear above each chapter aren't just random; they were the backdrop to my college years, marking moments of triumph and hard-earned lessons.

My college experience played out like a carefully curated soundtrack; the late nights, the hard lessons, the moments that shaped who I was becoming, all accented by the music that defined my era. However, while the titles may fit the themes, *I'm not telling you to live by the lyrics*. Instead, think of them as reminders of challenges faced, obstacles overcome, and the journey itself.

Soon, you'll be curating your soundtrack. The fact that you're reading this already demonstrates initiative. You're resourceful. You've got what it takes. I'm confident that you'll survive college and learn how to truly enjoy the experience.

"Ambitionz Az a Ridah"
Roots

> *"Resilience doesn't begin in college. It's already been developing in neighborhoods where survival is the daily curriculum; in homes where love stretches beyond resources. This foundation is what makes you ready for what's next."*

I grew up in Dayton, Ohio, in the inner city, not far from the Wright Brothers' original bicycle shop and the home of the famous poet Paul Laurence Dunbar.

Growing up in a Midwestern factory town shaped me in ways I'm still unpacking. I didn't have a clear picture of my future, but I knew one thing: I wanted more. I was a dreamer, not because I had access to the world, but because I didn't.

I came of age before the internet, so my imagination had to do the heavy lifting. My worldview was limited to TV shows, the pages of our neatly stacked encyclopedias, and the few things I saw outside my front door. And what I saw wasn't always hopeful.

Our community, though rich in pride, was weighed down by the residual effects of poverty, crime, drugs, and violence. We didn't talk about it much, but we lived it. That tension between what was and what could be stirred something in me.

Without money for travel or mentors who had "made it," I leaned on creativity. I imagined other places, other lives. That inner vision became my escape and, eventually, my direction.

When it came to college, though, I had no roadmap. I was a kid from the inner city who had only ever existed in predominantly Black spaces; my school, my neighborhood, my church. No one in my family had attended a four-year university, just the local community college.

College felt like a world apart. And I was just trying to find the door.

We had two HBCUs nearby (Central State, Wilberforce) and a PWI (Wright State), but I didn't personally know anyone who had gone to any of them. My only real reference points for college life were what I saw on TV and in movies: *School Daze* (1988), *Higher Learning* (1995), and *A Different World* (1987-1993). Those shaped my perception of college until I experienced it for myself.

THE DOOR I DIDN'T WALK THROUGH

In middle school, my mother found a free program for me called Wright STEPP (Science, Technology, and Engineering Preparatory Program). It was designed to prepare at-risk and underrepresented minority students for college, particularly in STEM. If they pursued a STEM degree, graduates received four years of tuition-free enrollment at Wright State University.

I loved the hands-on experiments and became curious about mechanical engineering. However, I eventually grew tired of sacrificing my summers and stopped attending. I didn't recognize the value of what I had. In my mind, Wright State was too close to home, and that didn't fit into my plan of escaping my environment. Looking back, I realize I walked away from a life-changing opportunity that could have left me debt-free.

I share this so you can learn from my mistake. Sometimes, the blessing you've been praying for doesn't come in the package you expected.

THE COLLEGE DECISION

By the time I hit high school, I still didn't have a real plan for college. I only had two schools on my radar: an HBCU (Southern University) and a PWI (Ohio State University). I was utterly clueless about the application process, and this was back when everything had to be submitted via paper and mailed in.

Thankfully, my high school guidance counselor stepped in. She helped me navigate deadlines, forms, and all the fine print I didn't even know to look for.

> *Life lesson: Don't be afraid to ask for help. Sometimes, the right people show up just in time.*

As much as the idea of going out-of-state excited me, deep down, I couldn't bring myself to leave my bedridden mother and aging grandmother. Staying closer to home felt like the right move. Ohio State had accepted me, offered a little financial aid, and was only about 60 miles away. It felt like the best of both worlds.

But let me tell you, nothing could have prepared me for the culture shock that was waiting on the other side.

"Changes"

The Awakening

"College is where the map ends and your real journey begins. At a PWI, that journey will test your resilience. Navigate it with purpose."

REALITY CHECK

I'd been to Columbus before for family trips, but had never seen the Ohio State campus. As orientation approached, I realized I had no clue how to get there. My mother had recently suffered a stroke and was now quadriplegic, which meant I was on my own. I had just turned 18 and had never driven on the highway.

Keep in mind that this was before GPS and smartphones. So, I went to AAA, had them highlight a route on one of those old-school paper maps, and hit the road in my beat-up car, nervous but determined.

As overwhelming as it was, that drive was a lesson in resilience. I made it safely, but as soon as I stepped onto campus, I was hit with another wave of overwhelm. This place was massive!

I eventually found my way to orientation. I sat alone, chip on my shoulder, trying to take it all in. Most of the other students had parents by their sides, but I didn't.

As I scanned the buildings, the people, the possibilities, I let myself drift for a moment, just long enough to whisper in my mind, *"I made it."* Coming from where I came from, that moment of pride felt sacred.

But then the speaker said something that snapped me right back to reality:

"Look to your left. Now, look to your right. One of you won't be here when you graduate."

At the time, it felt cold. Callous. Unnecessary. But I would soon learn how real it was. Between weed-out classes, financial stress, and the unspoken weight of navigating a space where I was often the only Black face in the room, many students like me didn't make it to the finish line.

That warning about not making it to graduation day stayed with me. It planted fear and determination in my spirit as I left orientation that day. Looking back now, it was the moment everything shifted; when college transformed from an abstract dream into a stark reality I had to navigate. The path ahead would test everything I thought I knew about myself, education, and what it meant to exist in spaces that weren't designed with me in mind. My real education was about to begin.

A WHOLE NEW WORLD

Move-in day finally arrived. It was my first time truly living away from home, and I was paired with a white roommate. Here I was, coming from an all-Black upbringing, now sharing a small space with someone from a small town with little exposure to Black people. When his parents helped him move in, his dad's face told me everything I needed to know.

I sighed, realizing this was going to be an *interesting* journey.

At first, I kept my distance. When I'd see my roommate on campus, I wouldn't even acknowledge him. It wasn't personal; it was just that I had no experience interacting with people outside of my community. I didn't know how to balance being myself while navigating a space where I was in the minority.

However, over time, I learned that I could be myself and still be open to others. My roommate was really cool, and we had some of the most eye-opening conversations about race and culture. Those talks helped me understand different perspectives and, more importantly, how to navigate spaces that weren't built with me in mind.

THE LESSONS I WISH I KNEW

Fast-forward to today. I'm an adult with my kids in college. Watching them navigate their experiences makes me reflect on my journey. I remember writing my four oldest sons a long email entitled *The 10 Commandments of College*, outlining all the things I wish I had known. As the years went on, I also shared it with some young men I mentored. Those emails eventually evolved into this book.

If you've ever heard of *What to Expect When You're Expecting*, you know it's one of the most comprehensive guides to pregnancy, yet it still can't cover everything. Similarly, this book won't give you the answer to every challenge you'll face in college. Instead, consider it advice from a concerned uncle, giving you enough insight to help you navigate unfamiliar waters without being blindsided. And most importantly, offering encouragement.

FINAL THOUGHTS

This book is written from the perspective of someone who lived on campus, but I know that's not the path for everyone. Maybe you're starting at a junior college to save money before transferring. Maybe you're commuting to a university nearby to cut down on room and board costs.

Whatever your situation:

- Don't let it make you feel "less than."
- Most of the principles in this book still apply, with minor adjustments.
- Your journey is *yours*. And I promise you, it *can* be done.

College isn't just about books and grades; it's about knowing how to move. You're stepping into a world where you might be the only one who looks like you in the room, where your culture might be misunderstood, and where you'll have to work twice as hard just to be seen as equal.

But don't trip, I got you.

This book is your playbook. From finding your people to handling adversity, from academic survival to mental wellness, I'm giving you everything I wish I had known. In these pages, you'll learn how to stay ready so you never have to get ready, how to build your network, navigate a space that wasn't built for you, and most importantly, win on your own terms.

The path ahead requires preparation, but before we outline specific strategies, let's get something clear...

"Letter to the President"

Setting the Stage

Setting the Stage

"Before you start this journey, understand the challenges ahead and how to move smart!"

To My Young Kings and Queens,

Before we dive into the thick of things, let's get something straight: college ain't for everybody. And that's okay. Let's start there.

If you don't go to college, don't ever feel less than. Success isn't limited to a degree; it's about making a choice that sets you up for a sustainable future. After high school, you have four options:

- ***College:*** Whether it's a PWI or an HBCU, go where it makes financial sense.

- ***Trade School / Community College + Working :*** A great path with less debt and practical skills.

- ***The Military:*** Offers structure, discipline, and tuition benefits if you play it smart.

- ***Entrepreneurship / Creative Hustles:*** Whether you're building a brand, selling a product, becoming an influencer, or monetizing a skill, this path requires vision, consistency, and grind, but it can pay off in powerful ways.

All four paths can lead to a future with stability and opportunity. The key is making a decision and then putting in the work to make it pay off.

TAKE OWNERSHIP

Some high schools, like mine, don't have a plethora of resources to prepare you for college. That's not your fault. But there are still things within your control that can change your trajectory.

When my kids gripe about their classes, I remind them that grades still matter. Not because they measure intelligence (they don't), but because they open doors. If you want scholarships, internships, and the ability to choose your path, you have to play the game. Sacrifice now so you can play later!

The reality is that we have to do twice as much to get half. That's a hard truth that likely won't change soon, but knowing the game gives you an advantage in moving more wisely.

THINKING ABOUT COLLEGE? HERE'S HOW TO START

1. Figure Out What You Want to Do

- You don't have to have your entire future mapped out; just identify a general direction that interests you, such as business, healthcare, technology, education, the arts, sciences, etc.

- Take a moment to reflect on your strengths and what you genuinely enjoy. What classes do you look forward to? What activities energize you? These can provide clues about potential paths.

- Aiming in a general direction makes it easier to pivot later, as opposed to having no direction at all and having to rebuild from scratch. Remember that many students change their majors during college, so this is just your starting point, not a lifetime commitment.

2. Make a List of Minimum 10 Schools

- Use Google & YouTube. Research the cost of attendance, room & board costs, majors offered, weather, activities, clubs, campus culture, and the treatment of Black students (yes, you can find all this information online).

- Create a spreadsheet (Google Sheets is free) and add all you discovered in your research into columns. This will make it easier to compare visually.

- Visit the school's website, navigate to the admissions page, and look for a 'Request Information' form or link. Fill in your contact details and select the majors that interest you. Most colleges will mail brochures about their programs, admission guides, and occasionally details about scholarships and financial aid. Sometimes, seeing the school colors, flipping through the majors, and holding something tangible in your hands is the moment it clicks and sparks the belief that college is within reach.

3. Complete the FAFSA

- The FAFSA (Free Application for Federal Student Aid) determines how much financial aid is available to you. Complete this as soon as possible after October 1st of your senior year, as some aid is first-come, first-served.

- Try to complete as much of the form as you can before asking your caregiver to provide tax information. It's good for you to learn about this process anyway, as you'll need to complete it each year of college.

4. Set Up a Common App Account

- The Common Application (Common App) is an online portal that allows you apply to multiple colleges simultaneously, saving time, energy, and stress. Create your account in the summer before senior year to get a head start.

- The platform simplifies the application process by allowing you to enter your information once and use it for all participating schools. Over 900 colleges and universities accept the Common App, making it an essential tool in your college application journey.

5. Write Your Essays

- Begin writing your essays early, ideally during the summer before your senior year. Use Google Docs as it's free, autosaves, and is easy to share with others for feedback. When complete, ask your advisor, English teacher, or another adult you trust to review.

- Many colleges ask similar questions, so you can often reuse and tweak essays for different applications. Keep a master document of all your essays to stay organized.

- Schools remember stories, not just stats, so make it personal. What experiences have shaped you? What challenges have you overcome? What makes your perspective unique? Give yourself time for multiple drafts; your first attempt is rarely your best.

THINGS TO KEEP IN MIND

Everyone moves through this process differently. Some of you will need hand-holding, and that's fine. Some of you will take charge, and that's fine too. No approach is right or wrong; just be ready to pivot when needed.

The journey is not about perfection, it's about progress.

- Guide yourself, but don't be afraid to ask for help.
- Don't feel like a failure if the road gets bumpy or you have to take a detour.
- Stay focused on the long game; how you finish matters more than how you start.

Refer to the First Year Preparation Checklist in Appendix B to ensure you start college on the right foot.

NOW THAT YOU'RE IN… HERE'S HOW TO MOVE

Alright, so you made it to campus. Congrats! But listen; just because you got here doesn't mean you're done learning. Now, let's talk about how to make the most of this experience, starting with something people don't tell you before moving in.

Basic hygiene.

Yes, I'm serious. You'd be surprised how many people need this conversation.

"All Eyez on Me"
Hygiene & First Impressions

LESSON I

"First impressions matter. Stay fresh, stay clean, and let your presence speak before you do."

> YOUR APPEARANCE COMMUNICATES BEFORE YOU SPEAK. MAKE IT SAY WHAT YOU INTEND.

Let's get this out of the way: hygiene is not optional. If you don't have a solid self-care routine before stepping on campus, life will humble you quickly. Nobody wants to be the person folks whisper about because you're musty, ashy, or walking around with a bird's nest on your head.

College is where you truly fine-tune your self-care game before entering adulthood. And since Black hair and skin require different levels of care than other races, you must know what works for *you*.

This chapter isn't about shaming anyone; it's about making sure you walk into any room looking, smelling, and feeling like you've got your life together. So, let's get into it.

HAIR CARE: YOUR CROWN DESERVES RESPECT

Whether you've got 360 waves, locs, an afro, or a protective style, your hair requires maintenance. What worked when you were younger (or what your mom handled for you) might not cut it anymore.

Black hair needs moisture. That means using water-based products, leave-in conditioners, and avoiding things that dry your hair out (like washing it every day with harsh shampoos). If you're clueless, don't stress, there's no shame in asking for help. Contact your siblings, parents, other family members, barbers, stylists, or even YouTube University.

For the Fellas:

- If you're rocking waves, moisturize, brush, and wrap it up at night.
- If you have locs or an afro, keep it clean, hydrated, and trimmed.
- If you have a fade, keep your lineup fresh. A sharp cut can make a $10 T-shirt look like a designer fit.

For the Ladies:

- Learn your hair type (3C, 4A, 4B, 4C - Google it). It'll save you from using the wrong products.
- Protective styles are your friend, but don't forget to take care of your real hair underneath.
- Edges matter; treat them with respect, and don't let anybody snatch them prematurely ;-)

You are royalty, treat your image like it. Don't let comfort make you careless. Presentation matters more than you think.

SKIN CARE: ASHY AIN'T IT

Look, we don't have the luxury of walking around dry and nobody noticing. Ashy skin is tacky, especially since it's easily preventable. That said, different people have different skin types, so it's important to figure out what works for *you*.

Basic Rules for Everybody:

- Lotion is non-negotiable. Keep a travel-size bottle on you; knees, elbows, and hands should never be ashy.

- Face soap and body soap are *not* the same. Dove bar soap is lovely, but if your face breaks out, you might need a real cleanser.
- Drink water. Your skin will thank you.

For the Fellas:

- If you shave, use a proper razor and avoid dry shaving unless you want razor bumps for days.
- If you have a beard, treat it like it's a valuable asset. Beard oil, conditioner, and a comb will keep you from looking scruffy.

For the Ladies:

- Makeup wipes are *not* skincare. Wash your face correctly.
- If you wear foundation, find one that matches your skin tone (your friends should not have to lie to you).
- Exfoliate, but don't overdo it, especially if you have sensitive skin.

Dealing with Eczema:

If you struggle with persistent dry, itchy, or flaky skin, you might be dealing with eczema; a common skin condition that affects many people. Sometimes what looks like being "ashy" is actually a medical condition that needs different care:

- Stick to gentle, fragrance-free products and avoid harsh soaps
- Moisturize regularly, especially right after shower-

ing while skin is still damp

- Don't scratch when it itches (pat the area or apply a cool, damp cloth instead)
- Keep your nails short to prevent damage from unconscious scratching
- Take lukewarm (not hot) showers and pat skin dry instead of rubbing
- Try to identify your triggers (certain fabrics, stress, or products that make it worse)
- If it's severe or persistent, campus health services can help with treatment options

SMELLING GOOD IS A LIFESTYLE

There is absolutely no reason for you to smell like roadkill. Personal hygiene isn't just about looking good; it's about *not offending people's noses.*

Bathe:

- I can't stress enough how easy it is to develop bad habits when you're away from home. Please—*please*—shower daily. If you hit the gym, double up. Your classmates will thank you.
- Thoroughly clean your pits and privates. Non-negotiable.
- Don't forget to clean the inside of your ears, as well as around them. You don't want a chunk of wax or other material hanging from your ears.
- Use a fresh towel regularly. A moldy towel can instantly ruin your clean shower.

Scent Strategy:

- Deodorant: Find one that works for you and has a pleasant scent. Apply it to *clean* underarms.

- Cologne/perfume: A good scent can make people remember you for all the right reasons. *Do not bathe in it.* Use one or two sprays max. You're trying to attract people, not gas them out.

- Remember that scent should be discovered, not announced. If people can smell you from across the room, you've gone too far.

BREATH CHECK

Along with monitoring your body odor, always be cognizant of your breath. A quick cup of your hands and breath check can make the difference between a good impression and being offensive.

You might have something important to say or be vibing with someone you're interested in, but if your breath is awful, they're only thinking about how to end the conversation. It can kill the moment, no matter how fresh you look. And the worst part? Most people won't tell you when there's a problem.

Mouth Maintenance Plan:

- Brush your teeth at least *twice* daily, morning and night, no excuses. Get all surfaces: fronts, backs, tops, and don't neglect your tongue (that's where a lot of the funk hides).

- Floss every night. Those food particles stuck between your teeth? They're decomposing in your mouth. That's nasty.

- Mouthwash isn't just for the minty feeling; it reaches places your toothbrush can't. Find one without alcohol if it burns too much.

Lifestyle Factors:

- Stay hydrated. Dry mouth = bad breath
- Smoking and vaping will give you dragon breath. If you must do it, be aware that everyone will be able to smell it on you afterward.
- What you eat affects your breath. Heavy garlic, onions, and certain spices will follow you around. If you indulge, have a plan in place.
- Digestive issues and bowel problems can negatively impact your breath. When your gut isn't right, it shows up in your mouth. Chronic bad breath might signal digestive issues that need medical attention.
- Certain medications can cause dry mouth or directly affect your breath. If you're on regular meds and notice persistent breath issues, talk to your doctor about solutions or workarounds.

The Emergency Kit:

- Keep mints or sugar-free gum in your backpack. Consider it part of your daily carry, just like your phone and keys.
- Travel-sized mouthwash or breath spray can save you during long days on campus.

Remember, nobody will tell you when your breath is offensive; they'll just create distance. Do yourself a favor and keep your mouth game as fresh as the rest of you.

DRESSING FOR THE OCCASION

Your wardrobe doesn't have to be expensive, but it should be clean, appropriate, and put together. You never know when you'll need to make a good impression; professors, job recruiters, and potential mentors all notice how you carry yourself.

Golden Rules:

- Wear clothes that fit. Baggy jeans and skin-tight shirts ain't it. Find a happy medium.
- Iron your clothes. Wrinkles make you look like you just rolled out of bed.
- Have at least one professional outfit. You don't need a three-piece suit, but you should have something for job interviews, presentations, and networking events.

And fellas, sagging isn't a style. Especially once you learn the origin, let's please retire that one.

MOVE SMART: ACTION STEPS

- Create a personalized hygiene routine including hair care, skin care, and daily maintenance.
- Make a checklist of essential personal care products appropriate for your hair and skin type.
- Build a "first impression" wardrobe with at least one professional outfit for presentations and interviews.
- Establish a laundry and room cleaning schedule to maintain your space and appearance.

FINAL THOUGHTS: MAKE HYGIENE A HABIT

College is the training ground for adulthood. The habits you build now will carry over into the real world.

- Start and stick to a self-care routine.
- Ask questions if you're unsure about hair or skincare.
- Keep your hygiene in check every single day.

One day, you may have your own family, and how your children present themselves is a direct reflection of their parents. You know you've seen someone unkempt before and wondered about their upbringing. In our community, we take pride in maintaining proper hygiene and presentation; it's an integral part of our legacy. That standard of excellence extends from childhood into adulthood. You'll always be somebody's child representing your family name, so honor that legacy and present your best self every day.

When you look good, you feel good. And when you feel good, you carry yourself differently. So, handle your business; your future self (and everyone who has to stand next to you) will appreciate it.

NEXT LESSON

Taking care of your physical appearance is the first step in presenting your best self, but there's more to the story than grooming and gear. Equally important is understanding how to maintain your cultural identity in spaces that weren't built with you in mind. Let's talk about staying grounded in who you are while navigating new environments...

"Only God Can Judge Me"
Cultivating Identity & Spirituality

LESSON II

"Stay grounded in who you are. Your culture and faith will be your anchor in unfamiliar spaces."

> YOUR IDENTITY IS YOUR FOUNDATION. STRENGTHEN IT DAILY, ESPECIALLY WHEN TESTED.

College is a microcosm of life, a test run for the real world. You take everything you learned at home, mix it with what you experience on campus, and somewhere in between, you figure out who you are. But make no mistake, college will challenge your identity.

For the first time, you're in an environment where people don't know you or your background. Some folks will be cool, some will be ignorant, and some will straight-up try to test you. That's why it's crucial to stay grounded in your spirituality, your Blackness, and your values.

DO NOT COMPROMISE WHO YOU ARE

You don't have to walk around campus in a "Black Power" hoodie daily. You don't have to argue with every ignorant person you meet. You don't have to prove your Blackness to anyone. But you do have to stay true to yourself.

Some people let higher education strip them of their identity. They start code-switching so hard they don't recognize themselves. They abandon their roots to "fit in." *Don't let that be you.*

Your heritage is the source of your strength, ambition, creativity, and resilience. Own it. And understand that staying true to yourself doesn't mean you can't grow, evolve, or connect with people from different backgrounds; it just means you don't have to lose yourself in the process.

SPIRITUAL HEALTH – STAYING GROUNDED

Whether you grew up in the church or are simply trying to figure out your spiritual path, don't neglect your spiritual health. College will test you mentally, physically, and emotionally. You need something to keep you centered.

Ways to Stay Connected Spiritually:

- Find a local church or faith-based student organization.
- Be routine with your prayer life; whether that's morning prayer, meditation, or journaling.
- Keep in touch with family or elders who keep you accountable in your faith.
- Set boundaries. Some people will try to challenge your beliefs just because they can. *You don't owe anyone an explanation for what keeps you grounded.*

Thankfulness and Gratitude

You've probably heard the saying, *"Your attitude determines your altitude."* However, the more profound truth is that your spiritual health is often shaped by how you choose to perceive your circumstances.

When life hits you with a setback, like failing a test or an unanswered prayer, it's easy to spiral into panic or frustration. But instead of stewing in that moment, you have another option: shift your perspective. Choose to see every loss as a lesson; every challenge as a setup for growth. You change your perspective in two ways.

First, utilize what's available to you. I once heard someone say, *"Somebody would be winning with what you've got."* That hit me hard. We often complain about what we lack, but someone else could take the very resources we ignore and turn them into success. Never take your college experience for granted. Somebody somewhere is praying for the opportunities you now have.

Second, recognize that gratitude shifts everything. It changes your outlook, strengthens your spirit, and even influences the atmosphere around you. Cultivating a thankful heart isn't just good advice; it's a spiritual practice. According to Philippians 4:6, gratitude in your prayer life has the power to alleviate anxiety and bring about peace.

So pause, take inventory, and give thanks, because a grateful heart makes room for greater things. Your spiritual health flourishes through daily practice and genuine connection, not just as a last resort during challenging moments. Nurture these habits now to build a foundation that sustains you throughout your college journey and beyond.

POLITICAL & SOCIAL AWARENESS

By the time you graduate, your political and social views will probably evolve. That's normal. You'll meet people with perspectives you've never considered before. But let's be clear; being open to learning doesn't mean letting people gaslight you.

Know What You Stand For:

- You don't have to argue with everyone, but you should at least know your history.

- Stay informed; read, listen, and ask questions. (Social media doesn't count as a reliable news source.)

- Just because someone is "nice" doesn't mean they aren't problematic. Be mindful of microaggressions and coded language.

Engaging Without Losing Yourself:

Some people love debating for sport. They'll try to bait you into arguments about race, politics, or religion just to see how you react. You don't have to engage in every discussion, especially if:

- The person isn't listening to understand, just to argue.
- You're feeling drained or disrespected.
- The topic is triggering or deeply personal.

It's okay to say, *"I'm not having this conversation with you."* Protect your energy!

ETHNIC PRIDE WITHOUT ASSIMILATION

Some folks step onto a PWI campus and immediately try to erase every trace of their Blackness. They downplay their culture, avoid Black spaces, and start parroting opinions just to "fit in." Why? Because sometimes Blackness makes people uncomfortable, and some people don't want to deal with that discomfort.

You Don't Have to Dim Your Light:

- If you grew up in an expressive household, don't let people make you feel like you have to shrink.
- If you love Black music, culture, and history, embrace it.
- If you have a name that people struggle to pronounce, correct them; don't let them rename you.

Being Black is not a burden, it's a privilege. Some folks will get it. Some won't. Either way, don't ever apologize for being who you are.

NAVIGATING CONVOS & SETTING BOUNDARIES

College will introduce you to people from all walks of life. Some will become lifelong friends. Others… not so much. It's important to know when to engage and when to walk away.

Personality Types You Might Run Into:

- *I Don't See Color* – A person who avoids conversations about race by claiming they don't see color. They refuse to acknowledge racism as it makes them feel uncomfortable.

- *You're One of the Good Ones* – Someone who tests boundaries by saying questionable things to gauge what they can get away with in your presence.

- *Debate Me* – Armed with half-truths from unreliable blogs and fringe content, they're quick to argue but refuse to acknowledge the ripple effects of systemic racism. Rarely, if ever, do they listen to understand.

- *Curious but Clueless* – Genuine, but uninformed. They want to learn, but often ask questions in ways that show a lack of context or awareness.

You don't have to entertain every conversation. Sometimes, the best response is to exit the chat. And hear me when I say you don't have to be the Black representative for every classroom discussion. If the topic of slavery, Jim Crow, or civil rights comes up, you are NOT obligated to be the spokesperson. If you want to speak, cool. If not, that's cool too.

MOVE SMART: ACTION STEPS

- Research and connect with a campus faith group that aligns with your values
- Create a list of personal boundaries that help you maintain your identity and values.
- Identify three cultural events to attend this semester that celebrate your heritage.
- Journal about your expectations, fears, and hopes for maintaining your identity at a PWI.

FINAL THOUGHTS: YOUR IDENTITY

You will grow in college, but growth doesn't mean forgetting who you are. Stay connected to your roots, stay spiritually grounded, and never let anyone make you feel like you have to erase yourself to belong.

- Be proud of where you come from.
- Keep your spiritual and mental health in check.
- Set boundaries and protect your peace.

At the end of the day, you define who you are; not your university, not your classmates, and definitely not society. So, walk in your truth, and never let anybody shake that.

NEXT LESSON

You've explored the importance of embracing your identity, even when it's not always welcomed. While staying true to yourself is essential, college isn't a solo journey. The connections you make now can shape not just your campus experience, but your entire future.

The people you let into your space can either build you

up or tear you down. Let's explore how to build relationships that will support your growth…

"Me and My Girlfriend"
Building Relationships

LESSON III

"Choose your circle wisely. Friends, mentors, and relationships can make or break your experience."

> THE CONNECTIONS YOU CHOOSE NOW SHAPE BOTH YOUR HAPPINESS AND YOUR FUTURE.

If lack of money is the #1 reason students don't finish college, relationships are a close second.

There's nothing wrong with love, friendship, or even a little fun. But if you let the wrong people into your life, you can get so caught up in drama, distractions, or heartbreak that your GPA starts looking like gas prices from the '90s.

College is a time to meet new people, expand your world, and learn about yourself, but don't lose yourself in somebody else. Prioritize your goals, build solid friendships, and keep your emotions in check.

RELATIONSHIPS: THEY CAN DERAIL YOU

Dating in College – Is It Worth It?

Look, I get it, college is full of new faces, new energy, and plenty of people who seem like they might be your future spouse. But here's the thing: you have the rest of your life to date, but you only have four years (or five… or six) to get this degree.

Some of us (you know who you are) get into relationships and suddenly forget why we're here. Next thing you know, you're skipping class to lie up in somebody's dorm. You're staying up late arguing with your situation-ship. You're so distracted by who's texting (or *not* texting) you back that your grades start suffering.

And for what? More often than not, the person you're

stressing over will do what's best for them, regardless. So, before you put someone above your education, ask yourself:
- Will this person support my goals or distract me?
- Are we both emotionally mature enough to handle a relationship?
- Are we on the same page spiritually? (Being equally yoked matters more than you think.)
- Am I prioritizing this relationship over my future?

If your answers are shaky, you already know what have to do.

Let's Talk About Abstinence

Abstinence is not lame. It's not old-fashioned. It's not weird. It's one of the most intelligent decisions you can make, especially in college. Choosing to wait, whether for spiritual reasons, emotional maturity, or just personal boundaries, is a form of self-respect and control.

Don't let anyone pressure you or shame you into protecting your peace. Your body isn't a negotiation tool; you don't owe anyone access to it just because you're dating or feeling a vibe.

- You're not "missing out"... you're staying focused.
- You're not "inexperienced"... you're intentional.
- You're not "less mature"... you're just not in a rush to risk your future for a temporary moment.
- You can be in love and still say, "Not right now."

Abstinence isn't about saying "no" forever. It's about saying "yes" to yourself first, and yes to a future where you're emotionally, spiritually, and mentally aligned with someone who truly respects you.

Sex: The Case for Waiting

Sex is not worth throwing away your future. Society's views on sex evolve with each generation. The goal here isn't to shame anyone; it's to ensure you graduate without unnecessary stress, drama, or financial consequences.

No sex is worth dropping out of school and potentially owing $37K + in student loan debt with no degree or viable way to repay it (I'll share a brief story on this in a minute). Not to mention, the spiritual bonds that are formed through cleaving to another are often challenging to break.

If you can wait, wait. No one ever ruined their life by NOT having sex. But plenty of folks have destroyed their lives by making reckless decisions.

If you absolutely cannot wait, then at least take some precautions:

- Buy contraceptives. If you're too embarrassed to buy condoms, you're not ready for sex.
- STIs are real. Get tested regularly, and don't assume someone is clean just because they "look" clean.
- If something happens, handle it. Don't ignore signs of an STI or an unplanned pregnancy. Most college clinics have resources; use them.

At the end of the day, your education is way more important than a temporary moment. Move wisely.

Sex: When You Don't Wait

Recall earlier when the orientation speaker said, *"Look to your left. Now, look to your right. One of you won't be here when you graduate."* Well, I was one of those individuals.

The race is not given to the swift, but once you veer off the path, it sure is a long, arduous journey back to the main road.

During my third year at OSU, my (now) wife and I found out we were expecting our first child. In an instant, my priorities shifted. I withdrew from school and took a third-shift job to support my family, determined that she would finish her degree on time. I refused to be the reason she didn't walk across that stage. My education was put on hold, but not forgotten. I made a promise to myself that one day, I'd return and finish what I started.

I'm proof that finishing school can still be done even when life throws you curveballs, but boy, is it a hard hill to climb once you have a family. I aim to keep it honest with you, so I will not glorify or sugarcoat it. Some deferred dreams leave permanent scars. We faced a lot of disappointment, heartache, and financial strain. I'm sharing this so you can learn from my experience rather than repeating it.

Don't get me wrong... I love my son (and all my children). And as hard as it was, I'm thankful my wife and I were resilient and stayed together (as opposed to a coparenting situation). He's now an adult and has graduated from college, but I still look back and wonder how different things might have been if he had been brought into a financially mature environment versus the struggle.

So heed my word, make life easier, and go a different path.

FRIENDSHIPS: CHOOSE YOUR CIRCLE WISELY

Some of the friendships you form in college will last a lifetime. Others? They'll fade as soon as the semester ends. And that's okay.

Real Friends vs. Fake Friends
- Real friends push you to be better, celebrate your wins, and hold you accountable.
- Fake friends bring drama, use you for what you can do for them, and disappear when you need them.

You don't have to be friends with everybody, but make sure the people in your circle genuinely want the best for you.

Platonic Friendships Are a Thing

Some of y'all have never had a genuine friendship with the opposite sex, and it shows. College is a great time to form platonic friendships; no strings, no ulterior motives, just genuine connection. And sometimes, these friendships will benefit you more than a relationship ever could.

Moral of the story? Build friendships with people who uplift you. Period.

ROOMMATES: HOW TO SURVIVE

Unless you have the luxury of living alone, you'll have to learn how to coexist with another person. And that can be a challenge.

How to Get Along with Your Roommate:
- Find common ground. Even if you're completely different, figure out something you can bond over.
- Set clear boundaries. What's off-limits? How do you feel about guests? Discuss these things early.
- Communicate like an adult. If something's bothering you, address it before it becomes a full-blown war.

When to Create Distance
Not every roommate situation will be perfect. If you can't get along, setting boundaries and keeping your distance is okay. Just be respectful. Passive-aggressive behavior only makes things worse.

PEERS: THE RIGHT PEOPLE
They say you are the average of the five people you spend the most time with. So if you're always around people who are lazy, reckless, or unmotivated... guess what? That energy will rub off on you.

How to Pick the Right Circle:

- Stick with people who want to see you win. Avoid people who don't care about their future, because they won't care about yours either.
- Cut off toxic energy early. If someone is always negative, draining, or dragging you into drama, let them go.
- Find people who inspire you. Surround yourself with folks who push you to be your best.

The people around you will either build you up or tear you down. Choose wisely.

MOVE SMART: ACTION STEPS

- List the qualities of healthy vs. unhealthy relationships to guide your connections.
- Identify spaces on campus where you can meet people with similar interests and values.
- Schedule regular check-ins with family and home-

town friends to maintain support networks.
- Create a boundaries document for dating relationships to reference when needed.

FINAL THOUGHTS: FOCUS ON WHAT MATTERS

College is about balance. Relationships, friendships, and social life all matter, but your education comes first.

- Prioritize your goals over temporary distractions.
- Build solid friendships and protect your peace.
- Make smart decisions about sex, roommates, and social circles.

You came here to get a degree, not a heartbreak, a toxic friendship, or an unexpected situation. Stay focused. Stay smart. And most importantly, choose your relationships wisely.

NEXT LESSON

The right relationships will uplift you, but even with a strong support system, you'll face challenges unique to being a Black student at a PWI. Let's talk about how to navigate those difficult moments with resilience…

IV

"Got My Mind Made Up"
Navigating Networks & Black Spaces

LESSON IV

"Find your tribe, be intentional about your connections, and move with purpose; make spaces that weren't built for you work for you."

> COMMUNITY IS CURRENCY. BUILD NETWORKS THAT WILL SUPPORT AND ADVANCE YOU.

College can feel like a social experiment, especially if you're Black at a PWI. You're surrounded by people from different backgrounds, trying to find your footing and figuring out where you belong.

Here's the reality: You need a network.

That doesn't mean you can't connect with people from all walks of life; you should. But you should never isolate yourself from your people. The Black community on campus may be small, but it's a lifeline. The bonds you build now will carry you long after graduation.

This chapter is about finding your tribe through Black student organizations, events, and, if you're interested, Greek Life.

BUILDING YOUR BLACK NETWORK

A PWI can sometimes feel like a different planet, especially if you're coming from a predominantly Black background. But here's the thing: You don't have to go through it alone.

The Black Student Union (BSU), cultural organizations, and Black campus groups aren't just clubs, they're community hubs. These spaces give you the chance to:

- Find friends who understand your experience
- Get support when things get tough

- Connect with mentors and professionals
- Stay plugged into Black culture on campus
- Learn about activism and Black student advocacy

If you're Black at a PWI, these events are where you'll see familiar faces, hear perspectives that reflect your own, and engage in conversations that matter.

Go to Everything!
The best way to stay connected? Show up. College is more than just class and studying, it's about building relationships and experiences that will shape you.

- ***BSU Game Nights & Socials*** – Meet people in a relaxed, fun environment.
- ***Special Speakers & Panels*** – Gain insight from Black professionals, alumni, and activists.
- ***Black Professional Organizations*** – Connect with Black professionals, business leaders, educators, and creatives who will be your future colleagues.
- ***Peaceful Marches & Silent Protests*** – Get involved in campus activism, whether it's supporting Black student concerns, diversity initiatives, or larger national movements.
- ***Black Church Groups*** – Your faith walk is important; these spaces can give you spiritual and emotional support.

Networking Within Your Major
Connecting with Black professionals and students in your field is a strategic move to build a supportive network,

gain mentorship, and access career opportunities. See *Appendix A* for a comprehensive list of 20 common majors among Black students and relevant professional organizations organized by major.

Engaging with these organizations can provide mentorship, professional development, and a sense of community, enhancing your college experience and paving the way for a successful career.

BLACK GREEK LIFE (THE DIVINE 9)

Even if you never plan to join a Black Greek Letter Organization (referred to as the Divine Nine or D9), you'll likely interact with them at parties, community service events, and through campus leadership.

The D9 consists of five fraternities and four sororities: Alpha Phi Alpha (ΑΦΑ), Alpha Kappa Alpha (ΑΚΑ), Kappa Alpha Psi (ΚΑΨ), Omega Psi Phi (ΩΨΦ), Delta Sigma Theta (ΔΣΘ), Phi Beta Sigma (ΦΒΣ), Zeta Phi Beta (ΖΦΒ), Sigma Gamma Rho (ΣΓΡ), and Iota Phi Theta (ΙΦΘ).

I suggest you attend at least one step show or probate ceremony so you can witness our cultural excellence in action. These traditions showcase the powerful combination of history, brotherhood/sisterhood, and artistic expression that's unique to Black Greek life.

A Different World

A family friend of ours had a son who grew up in a Black church, but he attended a predominantly white high school. Most of his exposure to Black culture came from Sunday mornings, not his day-to-day school environment. So when he got to college and told his parents he was thinking about "rushing" a fraternity, his mom immediately responded, *"Boy, if you don't rush your behind back to the Black part of campus!"*

It was amusing, but it also highlighted a deeper reality. For many students, especially those who have lived between cultural spaces, college can be the first time they're fully immersed in Black community life, whether through social organizations, cultural events, or Black Greek life.

That moment reminded me that sometimes, college isn't just about discovering who you are. It's about reconnecting with your roots. That story illustrates why it's important to understand the culture and traditions you're stepping into.

Know the Culture & Respect Traditions

Black Greek Life is its own world, deeply rooted in legacy, culture, and community. All these organizations go far beyond step shows and strolls/hops. They stand for service, scholarship, and lifelong brotherhood and sisterhood.

Now, a word about respecting traditions. There are some unwritten rules you should be aware of that can keep situations from going left:

- Don't wear their paraphernalia if you're not a member

- Don't cross their line when they're strolling

- Don't mimic their calls, hand gestures, or strolls

Is Greek Life For You?

If you're interested, find an organization that aligns with your values. Most importantly, make sure the people you'll cross with are the type you want to connect with. Joining a D9 organization can be life-changing, but it's not for everyone.

The Pros:

- Lifetime Brotherhood/Sisterhood and powerful

networking
- Cultural pride, historic legacy, and expanded social connections

The Cons:

- Significant financial and time commitments
- A demanding process that requires careful timing

Before committing, understand that pledging is mentally and physically demanding. Choose your timing carefully to preserve your academics, and always have at least one trusted confidant who knows what's happening for safety reasons.

Greek life offers respect, responsibility, and incredible connections, but it's *not* required for success. My goal isn't recruitment but education so that you can make the right choice for *you*.

MOVE SMART: ACTION STEPS

- Attend the first meeting of at least two Black student organizations within your first month.
- Research Black professional organizations in your field (see *Appendix A*) and join one
- Identify three potential Black mentors on campus or in your field of study
- Create a networking strategy to connect with at least one new professional contact monthly

FINAL THOUGHTS: FIND YOUR TRIBE

College is about relationships; who you connect with will shape your experience, opportunities, and even your sense of self. While you should network with all races, staying connected to your culture, your people, and your identity is just as important. If you only hang out with non-Black people, it starts to look like you're intentionally distancing yourself from your culture. That never bodes well for us in the long run.

There's a difference between being well-rounded and losing yourself to fit in, so make sure your circle reflects who you truly are.

- Get involved in Black student organizations, events, and professional networks.

- Surround yourself with diverse perspectives, but never feel you must distance yourself from your culture to succeed.

- If you're interested in black Greek life, research and move wisely.

- Whether you join a frat/soro or not, build strong relationships with mentors, friends, and allies who will support your growth.

You can navigate college alone, but why would you? Find your tribe, build your network, and make the most of these years.

NEXT LESSON

Learning to handle adversity builds character, but remember why you're here in the first place: to get that degree. Academics will test you in different ways, so let's break down how to excel in the classroom without losing your mind...

"Keep Ya Head Up"
Academic Discipline

LESSON V

"You will be tested academically. Stay focused, seek support, and outwork the system."

> COLLEGE REWARDS DISCIPLINE, NOT JUST INTELLIGENCE. DEVELOP SYSTEMS, NOT JUST KNOWLEDGE.

College is not high school. Your newfound freedom comes with a level of responsibility that will test your maturity and discipline in ways high school never did. This is an entirely different arena where the stakes are higher and expectations are greater.

There's no hand-holding, no reminders, and no extra credit just because you asked nicely. Professors don't chase you down for missing assignments. Nobody cares if you "meant" to turn it in. Either you handle your business, or you fall behind.

Your first semester sets the tone for your entire college career. If you build bad habits now, they will haunt you. If you slack off now, you'll be playing catch-up for years.

This chapter is about staying disciplined, developing strong study habits, and cultivating the mental resilience to persevere when challenges arise.

PART 1: THE IMPORTANCE OF DISCIPLINE

Many students struggle in their first semester, not because of intelligence (as you were smart enough to be accepted), but because of a lack of discipline. You don't get tardy notices or teachers following up with your parents if your grades drop. The new independence you have will take some adjustment.

What Makes College Academics Different?

- Professors don't chase you down. You're expected to keep up.
- Assignments take real effort. You can't BS your way through.
- Tests aren't always straightforward. Just memorizing notes won't save you.
- Falling behind is dangerous. One bad quiz can wreck your entire grade.

Academic discipline means checking your syllabus weekly, scheduling study time before you feel behind, and seeking help at the first sign of confusion; not the night before an exam.

Your First Semester is Make-or-Break

As an undergraduate, I found my classes to be quite challenging. I'd always been the guy who never had to study and could still grasp complex concepts at the last minute. Then I'd get my test scores back and couldn't understand why I bombed so badly. I'd get frustrated and want to blame the professor, my inner city schooling, anything to avoid looking inward.

And although some professors deserved criticism for their teaching methods (let's face it, some shouldn't be in classrooms), I eventually had to take ownership of my part in the grade and the hole I dug for myself. There were moves I could have made, but didn't because of stubbornness and a chip on my shoulder. I wasn't strategic at all. College was a game with rules that nobody taught me how to navigate. That doesn't have to be you.

Learn how to hold yourself accountable…

- Show up to class even if it's boring or attendance isn't required.
- Stay ahead on assignments.
- Build strong study habits.
- Recognize that procrastination can lead to your academic downfall and will hinder your success.

Bottom line? Take care of your business now so you won't regret it later. You have more control over your destiny than you realize.

PART 2: WEED-OUT CLASSES

Specific courses, especially in STEM majors, are designed to eliminate students. These are called weed-out classes because they're intentionally difficult to filter out students who can't keep up.

Why Do They Exist?

- Some programs only take the strongest students.
- Colleges want to boost their graduation stats. If you fail early, you don't make the school look bad later.
- Professors assume only the "serious" students will make it through.

How to Survive a Weed-Out Class

- Do not fall behind. Once you're lost, it's hard to catch up.
- Go to office hours early. Build a relationship with

your professor before you need help.

- Use tutoring services. Many campuses have free tutors; take advantage.
- Find a study group. The right people will help keep you accountable.
- Take bad grades seriously. If you bomb a quiz, IMMEDIATELY ask your professor what you need to do to pass.

If You Struggle, Speak Up Early

If you wait until the semester is almost over, it's too late. One bad quiz? Go to your professor. Ask about:

- Your current standing in the class
- Bonus work (if possible)
- Tutors or resources to help you catch up

Nobody's going to save you if you fail, but if you act fast, you can still turn things around.

PART 3: DEVELOPING STRONG STUDY HABITS

The biggest mistake students make? Thinking they know how to study when they really don't.

How to Study Effectively

- Instead of staring at notes for hours, try teaching the material to someone else
- Instead of cramming the night before, try spacing out study sessions over time
- Instead of re-reading the textbook 50 times, try self-quizzing without looking at answers

The Power of Study Groups

Some students prefer studying alone, but the right study group can be a game-changer. If you find people who actually want to succeed, you can:

- Break down tough concepts together.
- Hold each other accountable.
- Get different perspectives on the material.

But let's be clear, study groups should be productive, not just social time. If your group spends more time joking than working, find another group.

You Can't Cram Anymore

In high school, you might've been able to study the night before and still pull off an A. That won't work in college. Your brain needs time to absorb information, so study regularly, even if it's just 30 minutes a day.

PART 4: MAXIMIZING ACADEMIC RESOURCES

Campus Learning Centers

College isn't just about attending class; it's about using every available resource. Most universities have robust academic support centers that many students never utilize. These centers offer free tutoring, study skills workshops, and personalized academic coaching that can mean the difference between struggling and thriving.

Don't wait until you're failing to seek help. Visit these centers during the first few weeks of class to introduce yourself, understand their offerings, and establish connections. Remember, your tuition and fees already cover these services; you're leaving money on the table by not using them.

Try to find tutors who understand your perspective and learning style when seeking tutoring. Some centers offer options to request tutors from similar backgrounds, which can be invaluable for Black students navigating challenging courses with minimal representation.

Library Resources Beyond Books

Your campus library isn't just a building with books, it's an academic powerhouse with resources most students never discover. Beyond the obvious study spaces, most university libraries offer:

Research consultations with subject-specific librarians can save you hours of frustration when working on major papers. These experts know shortcuts and databases specific to your field that Google can't access.

There are technology centers where you can borrow expensive equipment like laptops, cameras, recording devices, and specialized software without spending money.

Private study rooms that can be reserved online, giving you a dedicated space for group projects or intense solo study sessions away from distractions.

Make a point to get a personal tour from a librarian early in your first semester. The fifteen minutes you invest will pay dividends throughout your college career.

Digital Learning Tools

Today's academic landscape is digital, and knowing which tools to use gives you a competitive edge. Most universities provide free access to premium software and platforms that would cost hundreds of dollars otherwise.

Check your university's IT website for free software available to students. This often includes the entire Microsoft Office suite, Adobe Creative Cloud, statistical programs like SPSS, and specialized software for your major.

Beyond university offerings, tools like Google Drive for collaborative work, citation managers like Zotero for research papers, and focus apps like Forest for productive study sessions can transform your academic efficiency.

Don't overlook the power of your university's online learning platform. Beyond checking grades, these systems often contain study materials, practice tests, and discussion forums that can clarify complex concepts outside class hours.

Building Faculty Relationships

One of the most underutilized resources at any university is the faculty. Professors are not just there to lecture; they're potential mentors, recommendation letter writers, and gateways to opportunities like research positions and internships.

Thoughtfully building relationships with professors can be particularly valuable. Seek out faculty who demonstrate cultural competence and genuine interest in your success. This doesn't mean they need to look like you (though representation matters when available), but rather that they see and value your potential.

To make the most of office hours:

- Come prepared with specific questions about the course material
- Research the professor's work and ask thoughtful questions about their expertise
- Share your academic and career goals to open doors to mentorship
- Follow up with a brief email thanking them for

their time

For email communication, maintain professionalism. Use proper salutations, check spelling and grammar, and be concise. Your digital communication shapes their perception of your seriousness as a student.

When asking for recommendation letters, give professors at least 3-4 weeks' notice, provide your resume and the position details, and explain why you've chosen them specifically. This thoughtfulness makes it easier for them to write a strong letter.

Peer Academic Resources

Your fellow students are walking resources. The key is connecting with peers who complement your academic strengths and weaknesses.

Effective study groups aren't just friends hanging out with textbooks open; they're strategically formed teams with diverse learning styles and strengths. Seek out classmates who ask insightful questions, take good notes, or understand concepts you find challenging.

For Black students at PWIs, connecting with other Black students in your major can provide both academic support and cultural understanding. These peer relationships often evolve into professional connections that last well beyond graduation.

Supplemental Instruction (SI) sessions, peer-led study groups facilitated by students who previously excelled in the course, offer structured review in a less intimidating environment than office hours. These sessions can be particularly valuable for "weed-out" classes where the curve is steep.

Remember that teaching others is one of the most effective ways to solidify your own understanding. By participating in peer tutoring, whether as the tutor or the student, you're strengthening your grasp of the material while building valuable connections.

PART 5: MENTAL FORTITUDE & RESILIENCE

You Will Fail at Some Point, And That's Okay.

At some point, you're going to struggle. You might fail a test. You might bomb an assignment. It happens. What matters is how you bounce back.

- Don't shut down. One bad grade isn't the end of the world; fix it and move on.
- Ask for help. There's no shame in needing tutoring or extra support.
- Adjust your habits. If something isn't working, change your approach.

Dealing with Stress & Burnout

College can feel overwhelming. The workload, the pressure, the expectations; it all piles up. If you don't take care of yourself, you will burn out.

Ways to Protect Your Mental Health

- *Exercise regularly* - It boosts focus and reduces stress.
- *Take breaks* - Nonstop study is counterproductive.
- *Go to events & socialize* - You need balance.
- *Get enough sleep* - 3 hours a night isn't enough.

Balance is the Key to Long-Term Success

Some students work too hard and burn out, while others work too easily and fall behind. The key is finding the balance between work and rest. College is a marathon, not a sprint. Pace yourself.

- Prioritize your academics.
- Take care of your body and mind.
- Have some fun, but don't get lost in the distractions.

MOVE SMART: ACTION STEPS

- Complete the Four-Year Academic Planning Sheet (*Appendix B*) to map your educational journey and stay on track toward graduation.
- Identify your learning style and create a study strategy that works for you.
- Schedule regular study blocks in your calendar and treat them like appointments.
- Find and visit campus tutoring centers before you actually need help.

FINAL THOUGHTS: HANDLE YOUR BUSINESS

- Your first semester sets the tone, so start strong.
- Weed-out classes are designed to be hard; adjust accordingly.
- Develop strong study habits early; cramming won't cut it.
- Failing happens; what matters is how you recover.
- Balance academics, health, and social life to avoid burnout

ACADEMIC DISCIPLINE

At the end of the day, you're here to succeed. Nobody's going to do the work for you. Stay disciplined, stay resilient, and make every semester count.

NEXT LESSON

Your mental performance depends heavily on your physical well-being. Even with perfect study habits, neglecting your body will hold you back. Here's how to maintain your mental, physical, and emotional health while balancing everything else...

VI

"Holla if Ya Hear Me"
Healthy Living

LESSON VI

"What you do with your body affects how you feel, perform, and succeed."

> YOUR BODY POWERS YOUR MIND. PRIORITIZE HEALTH FOR ACADEMIC SUCCESS.

College is a breeding ground for bad habits. Late-night fast-food runs, skipping meals, energy drinks instead of water, sitting around all day… it catches up to you fast.

Ever heard of the Freshman 15? It's real. Beyond weight gain, your physical health affects everything: your energy levels, your focus, and even your mental health. If you feel sluggish, it's probably because of how you're treating your body.

This chapter isn't about turning you into a gym rat or a health nut. It's about simple ways to stay active, eat right, and enjoy the college experience without wrecking your body.

EATING RIGHT – AVOIDING THE FRESHMAN 15

Most college diets are terrible. You don't need to be a nutritionist, but you do need some basic eating habits to prevent fatigue, bloating, and weight gain.

Common College Eating Mistakes:

- Living off ramen and energy drinks / coffee
- Skipping meals then binge eating later
- Late-night fast food runs
- Treating the cafeteria like an all-you-can-eat buffet
- Eating the same fried foods from the cafe daily

Simple Rules for Eating Smart:

- Balance your plate. More protein and veggies, less fried and greasy food.
- Drink more water. Dehydration makes you feel tired and can be mistaken for hunger. If your daily intake is mostly soda and coffee, fix that.
- Don't skip meals. Your brain needs fuel, especially for those long study sessions.
- Watch the late-night snacking. Pizza at 2 AM on the regular will catch up to you.

College Meals That Won't Sabotage Your Body:

If you're broke and in a rush, here are quick, cheap meals that are better than instant ramen:

- Oatmeal + fruit (filling and cheap)
- Eggs + toast (protein & carbs = good energy)
- Peanut butter & banana sandwiches (easy, healthy, and affordable)
- Chicken & rice bowls (simple, meal-prep friendly)
- Protein shakes (great for a quick breakfast)

Eating better doesn't mean giving up junk food forever. It just means avoiding it as part of your diet.

FITNESS – STAY ACTIVE

Fitness matters in college. Staying active isn't just about looks, it's about:

- Energy levels – Exercise wakes you up better than caffeine.

- Mental health – Movement reduces stress and improves focus.
- Confidence – Feeling strong and capable affects how you carry yourself.

College is stressful, and your body needs movement. You don't have to train like an athlete, but you shouldn't be completely inactive either.

How to Stay Active Without Overthinking It:

- Use the campus gym. It's free (or already included in your fees), so take advantage.
- Walk more. If your class is a 10–15-minute walk away, take the scenic route.
- Take the stairs sometimes. Elevators are nice, but a little extra movement won't kill you.
- Stretch. Sitting all day is bad for your body. Loosen up.

JOIN INTRAMURAL SPORTS & REC ACTIVITIES

You don't have to be a varsity athlete to stay active. Intramural sports, club teams, and rec center activities are great ways to:

- Stay in shape.
- Meet new people.
- Have fun doing something competitive.

Options to Consider:

- Basketball, flag football, soccer, volleyball (low-commitment but fun)

- Martial arts or boxing clubs (good for fitness and self-discipline)
- Dance teams or fitness classes (Zumba, yoga, spin classes, etc.)

If you're not into sports, at least find something active you enjoy. Even if it's just walking, cycling, or doing bodyweight workouts in your dorm.

The goal is to move your body; your future self will thank you.

MAKE THE MOST OF COLLEGE SPORTS EVENTS

Go to Games – You Won't Regret It
Even if you're not into sports, attending a big college game is an experience. The energy, school spirit, and packed stadium are something you don't get anywhere else.

If your school has a strong sports program, splurge on a big game at least once. Rivalry games, homecomings, and championships are worth it.

Why It Matters:

- You're only in college once. Enjoy the full experience.
- It builds school pride (even if you don't care about the team).
- It's fun. Period.

If you don't care about sports, go for the social aspect; you might enjoy it.

MOVE SMART: ACTION STEPS

- Schedule a visit to your campus health center to learn about the available services.
- Create a weekly meal plan that includes proper nutrition within your budget.
- Identify physical activities you enjoy and schedule them 3-5 times weekly.
- Develop a sleep routine that gives you 7-8 hours of rest each night.

FINAL THOUGHTS: HEALTHY HABITS = SUCCESS

- Eat better so you don't feel sluggish and tired all the time.
- Staying active helps with focus, energy, and mental health.
- Intramural sports & rec activities are fun ways to stay in shape.
- Go to college sports, it's an experience you won't want to miss.

Your body and mind are connected. If you feel better physically, you'll do better academically. Take care of yourself.

NEXT LESSON

A healthy body and mind require proper support systems. Knowing which resources are available and using them can make the difference between struggling and thriving. Let's talk about how to maximize the tools at your disposal to lighten your load.

VII
"I Ain't Mad at Cha"
Resources & Support

LESSON VII

"Success isn't a solo mission. Use every resource available to stay ahead and stay strong."

> SUCCESS COMES TO THOSE WHO MAXIMIZE THEIR RESOURCES. YOU'RE ALREADY PAYING FOR MOST OF THEM.

College isn't just about being smart; it's about being resourceful.

You can be the most intelligent person in the world, but you will struggle unnecessarily if you don't use the tools around you. There are plenty of ways to make your life easier, but it's up to you to use them.

This chapter is about saving yourself from unnecessary stress by backing up your work, correctly obtaining your books, asking for help when needed, and learning how to bounce back from setbacks.

1. BACKING UP YOUR WORK

Let me tell you a quick story. My mother worked at a hospital, and one of the doctors gave me his 4-year-old Macintosh Portable when I went to college. It was 640 x 400 pixels, with 1MB of RAM, a 1.44 MB double-sided floppy drive, and a weight of 16 lbs. These were the AOL dial-up years. If you've Googled that dinosaur by now, you know it was riddled with issues.

One night, I spent hours grinding through an 8-page paper, my longest one at that point. Something in my gut kept telling me: *"Save your work. Back it up."* But I ignored that inner voice.

Guess what happened? The Mac froze, rebooted, and wiped out my entire paper. Gone. Just like that. I learned a hard lesson that night. Technology will fail you when you need it most.

How to Never Lose Your Work

- Use Google Drive. It auto-saves, so your work is safe even if your laptop crashes.
- Carry a flash drive. They're small, cheap, and life-saving.
- Email important files to yourself, just in case.
- If your gut tells you to save, LISTEN.

College papers, notes, and projects, back them up in at least two places. Your future self will thank you.

For a comprehensive list of digital tools and apps that can help you stay organized and productive, see Appendix A.

2. BUYING BOOKS SMART – DON'T GET ROBBED

College bookstores are predatory. In some cases you have no choice but to use them, but avoid them if possible. Here are other tips I wish I would've known:

Why You Shouldn't Buy Books Immediately

- Professors change their minds. Sometimes they list books but never actually use them.
- You might not need every book. Some classes rely more on lectures and handouts.
- There are cheaper alternatives. Buying directly from the bookstore is like paying full price at an airport; it's unnecessary.

How to Get Books for Cheap

- *Amazon & Chegg:* Buy, rent, or get used books for way less.
- *Book swaps & upperclassmen:* Ask around as someone might have the book from last semester.
- *PDF versions:* Some textbooks are floating online if you look hard enough.
- *Library copies:* If the book is expensive, check if your campus library has a copy on reserve.

The Strategy:

Wait until your syllabus is out. Attend the first class, see if the book is truly required, and then decide how to get it for the cheapest price possible.

Develop financial discipline by utilizing the College Budget Worksheet in Appendix B to track your income and expenses.

3. ASKING FOR HELP – DON'T BE TOO PROUD

Nobody cares if you're struggling unless you speak up. Many students fail simply because they're too scared to ask for help. But here's the truth:

- Professors are more likely to help students they know. If you've never spoken to them all semester, don't expect them to save you in Week 14.
- Tutors exist for a reason. Many schools offer free tutoring; USE IT.
- Your academic advisor isn't just a checkbox. They can help with degree planning, class selection, and career advice.

How to Build a Relationship with Your Professors

- Go to office hours BEFORE you're failing.
- Ask meaningful questions, not "Will this be on the test?"
- Show effort. Professors respect students who try.

The students who actively ask for help are the ones who succeed. Don't wait until you're drowning; get help early.

4. WHAT IF YOU FAIL A QUIZ?

Listen, failing happens. Even the best students bomb a test here and there. What matters is what you do next.

Steps to Take After a Bad Grade

- Check your syllabus. Figure out how much that quiz affects your final grade.
- Talk to your professor. Ask about bonus work, extra credit, or tutoring recommendations.
- Adjust your study methods. If what you're doing isn't working, change it up.
- Don't dwell, move on. One bad grade won't ruin your life unless you let it.

Dropping a Class – There's No Shame in It

Some students stay in a class they're clearly failing, thinking they can magically turn it around. That's a bad move.

- Know your school's deadline for dropping classes.
- If you're failing with no way to recover, consider dropping.

- A "W" (withdrawal) looks way better than an "F."

Failing a test can make you feel inadequate, but it doesn't define you. What you do next does.

5. PROFESSIONALISM & TIME MANAGEMENT

Don't Be Late
College is practice for the real world. Some habits you develop now will carry over into adulthood. That means *on time = early*. Conversely, *late = disrespectful*.

Professors and professionals notice who respects their time. Being habitually late tells people you're unreliable. If you commit, *show up* and *be punctual*. Class, work-study, and extracurricular activies all deserve the same respect. Being on time shows you take your commitments seriously.

Organizing Your Semester
If you're always missing deadlines or scrambling last-minute, it's time to get organized.

- Use a planner or calendar.
- Day 1 of class, write down every due date from the syllabus.
- Plan study sessions in advance.

Study Like It's Your Job
The students who treat college like a job are the ones who graduate on time. Block out time for studying just like you would for work, and don't rely on motivation - use discipline instead. You're human. Some days, you won't feel like studying, but do it anyway.

MOVE SMART: ACTION STEPS

- Complete the College Budget Worksheet (*Appendix B*).
- Set up backups for all critical documents.
- Research and apply for at least three scholarships this semester.
- Create a list of campus resources with contact information, locations, and hours.

FINAL THOUGHTS: RESOURCEFULNESS

Be resourceful. Be smart:

- Back up your work; technology will betray you.
- Don't buy books immediately.
- Ask for help early; pride will ruin you.
- If you fail a quiz, don't panic; adjust your approach.
- Time management and professionalism matter.

College success isn't just about intelligence; it's about knowing how to use the resources available to you. The students who thrive are the ones who do.

NEXT LESSON

With the right strategies for academics, wellness, and support, you're positioned to do more than just survive college. But what happens when things go left? Let's talk about safety, street smarts, and how to protect yourself on campus and off...

VIII

"So Many Tears"

Staying Safe

LESSON VIII

"Protect your peace, health, and future at all costs."

> ONE MOMENT OF RECKLESSNESS CAN DERAIL YEARS OF PROGRESS. PROTECT YOUR FUTURE AT ALL COSTS.

College can be fun, but it can also be dangerous if you're not paying attention. People make dumb decisions in college. Some of them bounce back. Others? Not so much.

This chapter isn't here to scare you but to ensure you don't end up in a situation you can't walk away from.

Let's talk about how to stay safe, avoid unnecessary risks, and use the resources available to you.

1. DRUGS & ALCOHOL – JUST DON'T DO IT

I'm not going to sugarcoat this: Don't do drugs. Period. I don't care if you think you're "just experimenting" or "just trying it once." These days, you don't know what you're taking.

Why You Should Stay Away

- People lace stuff all the time. One hit of something laced with fentanyl? *Game over.*

- You don't know whom to trust. Just because someone seems cool doesn't mean they won't slip something in your drink.

- You can ruin your entire future in one night. Drugs don't just mess up your body; they mess up scholarships, job opportunities, and your freedom.

If You Choose to Drink, Be Smart About It

I'd rather you not drink at all. But if you do, you'd better be smart about it.

- NEVER drink from an open cup at a party or club. If someone hands you a drink, decline it. If you left your drink unattended? *Toss it and get a new one.*
- Keep a lid or cap on your drink. If it doesn't have one, hold it in your hand at all times.
- Drink slowly. *Sip. Don't chug.* You don't need to be the first one drunk at the party.
- Know your limit. If you feel off, stop drinking immediately.
- If you're uncomfortable, say NO. You don't owe anyone an explanation for protecting yourself.

Most importantly: If a situation feels off, *LEAVE.* Your safety > socializing.

2. PARTYING SMART – AVOIDING DANGER

College parties can be a good time or a disaster, depending on who you're with and how you handle yourself.

Golden Rules of Partying Safely

- Go out with people you trust. Not just random classmates, actual friends who have your back.
- Make a plan before you go. How are you getting there? How are you getting back? Don't assume you'll "figure it out."
- Watch out for each other. If one person is too drunk, feeling off, or uncomfortable, the whole group should leave.
- ALWAYS leave together. If you came as a group,

leave as a group.

Warning Signs to Leave a Party Immediately:

- People acting aggressively or weirdly. (Fights, tension, shady behavior)
- You feel like someone is watching you or following you.
- The vibe shifts from fun to uncomfortable.
- You see someone messing with drinks.
- Your gut tells you to go.

If something feels off, GET OUT. Your instincts are there for a reason. Trust them.

3. CAMPUS SAFETY – RISKY SITUATIONS

Let's talk about staying safe on campus and in your dorm. Just because you're in college doesn't mean bad things can't happen. And note, this advice is for both males & females.

How to Protect Yourself on Campus

- Never walk alone at night. If you have to, stay in well-lit areas and keep your phone in your hand (not your pocket).
- Know your campus emergency numbers. Most schools have campus police or security apps. Save them in your phone.
- Be aware of your surroundings. Walking with your headphones in, looking at your phone? That's how people get caught slipping.

- If you feel unsafe, don't hesitate to call for help. It's better to be paranoid than reckless.

Dorm Safety – Lock Up & Stay Smart

- Lock your doors. Don't assume your roommate will.
- Don't let random people into your dorm. Even if they "seem cool."
- Keep valuables hidden. Laptops, cash, and important documents should never be out in the open.

Remember: Just because you're on campus doesn't mean you're in a "safe bubble." Stay sharp.

For a comprehensive safety strategy tailored to your specific needs and campus, complete the Personal Safety Plan Template in Appendix B.

4. STUDENT HEALTHCARE – TAKE ADVANTAGE

You're Paying for It So Use It

Many students ignore campus health services because they don't realize what's covered. If you're paying tuition, chances are you have access to free or low-cost medical care.

- Doctor visits for illnesses, injuries, and check-ups
- Mental health counseling and therapy
- Sexual health services (STI testing, birth control, etc.)
- Prescription discounts for common medications

Don't Ignore Health Issues

If you're sick, GO TO THE DOCTOR. Don't just "tough it out." What starts as a minor issue can turn into a major problem.

If you're struggling with stress, anxiety, or depression? Get help. College is tough, and mental health is just as important as physical health.

The bottom line is to take care of yourself; your body and mind need it.

MOVE SMART: ACTION STEPS

- Complete the Personal Safety Plan Template (*Appendix B*).
- Program campus emergency numbers into your phone as favorites.
- Identify safe study spaces and transportation options for late nights.
- Find at least one trusted friend who can be part of your safety check-in system.

FINAL THOUGHTS: YOUR SAFETY

- Avoid drugs & be smart about drinking. If you're in an unsafe situation, LEAVE.
- Go out with people you trust & never leave your friends behind.
- Be aware of your surroundings. Crime happens on campus, too.
- Use student healthcare; it's there to help you.

Your safety is not worth risking for a party, a drink, or a good time. If something feels wrong, listen to your instincts and remove yourself. You only get one life. Protect it.

NEXT LESSON

Even when you move carefully, life still happens. The unexpected will show up, and you'll face challenges along this journey. Let's explore how to overcome adversity, bounce back, rebuild, and stay focused when things don't go as planned...

IX
"Hold Ya Head"
Handling Adversity

LESSON IX

"You will face challenges. Learn when to speak up, when to push back, and when to pivot."

> RESILIENCE ISN'T ABOUT AVOIDING CHALLENGES BUT DEVELOPING THE TOOLS TO OVERCOME THEM.

Life happens. The question is, how will you handle it when things don't go as planned? At some point, things will go left. Maybe you get stranded somewhere, find yourself in a bad situation, or hit a rough patch academically. The worst thing you can do? Stay silent out of fear.

This chapter is about moving wisely, knowing when to call for help, and understanding that as a Black student, you don't have the same safety nets as everyone else.

1. IF YOU'RE IN TROUBLE, CALL SOMEONE

You might be scared to make that call. You might think:

- "They're going to be mad at me."
- "I don't want to disappoint them."
- "I don't want to hear their mouth."
- "I can fix this myself."

Forget all that. If you need help, pick up the phone!

- Stranded at a party or out of town? Call someone.
- Got into legal trouble? Call a trusted adult immediately.
- Feeling unsafe? Leave first, explain later.

Stuff happens in life. Your loved ones would rather get a call at 2 AM than find out later that something went horribly wrong. Just try not to get yourself into something too deep.

2. "YOU CAN'T DO WHAT THEY DO"

This isn't about fear. This is about facts. You have to move differently. Some students can mess up and bounce back because their parents have the resources to clean it up. Expensive lawyers, connections, safety nets; we don't always have that luxury.

The truth:

- Black students are often judged more harshly for the same mistakes.
- The legal system is NOT on your side.
- Colleges protect their image before they protect you.

As a teen, I will never forget the worry in my mother's tone as she cautioned me, *"Jay you can't do what they do!"*

Although my mother would attempt to move mountains with her bare hands to make a way for me, I read her message loud and clear; our resources were limited if I got into serious trouble.

If your non-Black friends are wilding out, skipping class, experimenting with substances, understand that their reality isn't yours. You cannot afford to move recklessly. The consequences are different for you!

3. TRUST YOUR INTUITION – IT WILL SAVE YOU

Curiosity talks you into dumb situations. Intuition

talks you out. Have you ever felt that weird gut feeling before something goes wrong? Listen to it.

Red Flags to Leave a Situation:

- The energy shifts; people start acting differently.
- You feel like someone is watching you or setting you up.
- You're the only Black person in the room, and something feels off.
- People are pressuring you to do something you're uncomfortable with.

Your gut is your early warning system. If it doesn't feel right, LEAVE.

4. WHAT TO DO IF YOU'RE IN A BAD SITUATION

Stranded or Stuck?

- Call someone who can come and get you.
- Use rideshare apps, but only if you're with people you trust.
- Never wander alone at night. Stay in a safe, well-lit area.

Feeling Unsafe at a Party?

- Leave with your group. Never go alone.
- If someone is making you uncomfortable, remove yourself immediately.
- Don't be afraid to call for help.

In Legal Trouble?

- DO NOT try to "talk your way out of it."
- Ask for a lawyer before saying anything.
- Call a trusted adult immediately.
- Understand that staying silent is better than making the situation worse.

5. MENTAL & EMOTIONAL RESILIENCE

College will test you: academically, socially, and emotionally. There will be days when you:

- Doubt yourself.
- Feel overwhelmed.
- Wonder if you even belong.

How to Handle Stress & Setbacks

- Talk to someone: professors, mentors, counselors, family. Don't suffer in silence.
- Take a break when needed. Burnout is real.
- Focus on solutions, not just the problem. What's the next move?
- Remember why you're here. One setback does NOT define you.

If you're struggling, get help. Mental health services on campus exist for a reason. Use them.

MOVE SMART: ACTION STEPS

- Identify three trusted confidants you can call when facing challenges.

- Create a self-care routine for handling stress and difficult situations.
- Research campus mental health resources and save their contact information.
- Develop personal mantras or affirmations that help you stay resilient.

FINAL THOUGHTS: HANDLE ADVERSITY WISELY

There are ways to handle adversity wisely. Always remember:

- If you're in trouble, CALL SOMEONE. Don't suffer in silence.
- Move smartly, you don't have the same safety nets as others.
- Trust your intuition. If something feels off, leave.
- Don't give up if you fail or struggle; adjust and bounce back.

Life is unpredictable. The key is knowing how to handle it when things go wrong. Stay smart. Stay resilient. And if you need help, ask for it.

NEXT LESSON

You've faced setbacks, but you're still standing. Now it's time to thrive, not just survive. With the resilience to handle setbacks, you're ready to make the most of your college experience. Now, let's talk about how to create memories that will last a lifetime...

"Picture Me Rollin"
Seizing Opportunities

LESSON X

"Make sure you leave with more than just a degree."

> COLLEGE IS TEMPORARY, BUT ITS IMPACT IS PERMANENT. MAXIMIZE EVERY EXPERIENCE.

This is your moment, don't waste it. College is one of the few times in life when you get to focus on yourself, your growth, and your experiences, all while having a built-in safety net.

Yes, you're here to get a degree. But college is more than that. It's about the people you meet, the places you go, and the memories you create.

Many people never get this opportunity. So please don't take it for granted. This is the time to say yes to new experiences, step outside your comfort zone, and enjoy every moment while still handling your business.

Let's talk about how to make these years unforgettable.

1. CARPE PER DIEM – LIVE IN THE MOMENT

This is the last time in your life when you can be (mostly) carefree. After this? Bills. Jobs. Adult responsibilities.

- You worked hard to get here, so embrace it.
- Have fun, meet people, and try things you never thought you would.
- Make memories that will last a lifetime.

But... as I mentioned before, their fun is different from ours. Know your limits, move smart, enjoy yourself, but don't put yourself in situations that could derail your future.

2. TRY NEW THINGS

College is the perfect time to discover what you like, what you don't like, and what you're truly capable of. Step outside of your comfort zone.

- Take a class that challenges you. Even if it's not in your major, expand your knowledge.
- Try a new sport or activity. Intramurals, dance classes, weightlifting; find something active you enjoy.
- Go to events you normally wouldn't attend, such as comedy nights, poetry slams, and art exhibits, to expose yourself to different cultures and experiences.
- Buy souvenirs and keepsakes. School shirts, game tickets, and pictures will mean something years from now.
- Document everything. Take pictures, write down your experiences, and save mementos; this time will fly by faster than you think.

The more you experience, the more you grow.

3. TRAVEL IF YOU CAN – SEE THE WORLD

If you get the chance to study abroad, take it. Travel will stretch your thinking. You'll see life through a wider lens and come back more adaptable, independent, and open-minded. Just make sure you always travel with a sizable group.

If studying abroad isn't in the cards:

- Take a road trip with friends. Explore cities you've

never been to.

- Pull up to a legendary HBCU homecoming or Battle of the Bands, as they're cultural experiences you'll never forget.
- Check out major campus events at other PWIs. Some schools are known for their signature weekends, which attract students from all over.
- If there's a conference, retreat, or leadership event, go.

The world is bigger than your campus. Go see it. Go feel it.

4. BALANCE FUN & RESPONSIBILITY

Have fun, but don't forget why you're here. Try to find a healthy balance.

- Your education is your priority.
- Your health, physical and mental, comes first.
- Make smart decisions that won't come back to haunt you.

Yes, enjoy yourself, but handle your business so you can enjoy the rewards later. Never forget that we don't have the same safety nets, so move wisely.

5. LEAVE WITH NO REGRETS

When you look back on your college years, you don't want to say:

"I wish I had gotten involved."
"I should have built better connections."
"I regret not stepping outside my comfort zone."

You want to say:

"I took advantage of every opportunity."
"I built networks that will last a lifetime."
"I made the most of these years and am ready for what's next."

This is your time. Take the risk. Make the move. Enjoy the ride.

6. NAVIGATING BREAKS: HOME BALANCE

Let's say you've completed your first year of college. You've survived the highs and lows of independence, time management, and learning to structure your schedule. In this microcosm of adulthood called college, you've taken your first steps into growing up.

Now it's summer break, and returning home might feel… different. You've gotten used to your freedom, so adjusting to your parents' rules again may feel like a step backward. But here's the reality: while you were away discovering yourself, their lives kept moving too. Parenting doesn't stop just because you've been away, and even if you've earned more trust, most caregivers will still instinctively try to protect you.

The best thing you can do is show them how you've matured. Be helpful. Be respectful. Show growth. If you used to be selfish in high school, prove that you've leveled up. Your brain's still developing, but let your actions speak for how much you've grown. Make that summer so pleasant, they're a little sad to see you go back.

What if going home isn't an option? Not everyone can, or should, go home for the summer. Maybe the environment isn't safe. Maybe your relationship with your family is strained. Or maybe, financially, it just doesn't make sense.

If that's you, don't panic. I didn't know back then that many colleges offer summer jobs that let you stay on campus with free room and board, a meal plan, and even a little cash. It's a win-win; you get housing, food, and experience while ending the summer with some money in your pocket. These jobs can be competitive or hidden, so check campus job boards, talk to your RA, and ask your academic advisor or counselor.

Roles vary, from campus tour guides to RAs for summer programs to camp counselors for youth activities, but the key is positioning yourself early. Sometimes, staying on campus for the summer is the best move you didn't know you could make.

MOVE SMART: ACTION STEPS

- Create a college bucket list of experiences you want to have before graduating.

- Research study abroad, internship, or service-learning opportunities.

- Schedule exploratory meetings with professors about research opportunities.

- Plan one off-campus cultural or professional event to attend each semester.

- Take advantage of the scholarships and online communities listed in *Appendix C* to support your academic and personal growth throughout your college journey.

FINAL THOUGHTS

From your first day on campus to your summer breaks and eventually graduation, every experience shapes your journey. As you move forward with these strategies, remember...

The future starts now...

- Say yes to opportunities.
- Take risks (the smart kind).
- Meet people, explore, and create memories.
- Make every experience count.

Because once this chapter of your life is over, you can't get it back.

LAST LESSON

Carpe Per Diem. Seize the day.

"ME AGAINST THE WORLD"
Closing Comments

CLOSING COMMENTS

"Your journey doesn't end here. Take what you've learned and keep building your legacy."

YOUR BLACKNESS IS NEVER IN QUESTION
Let me reiterate... choosing to attend a PWI does not make you any less Black.

Maybe you chose a PWI because...

- It was closer to home.
- It offered more scholarship money.
- A sibling or mentor went there, and you were familiar with it.

Whatever the reason, it's YOUR decision. Some people will try to make you feel like you should have gone to an HBCU instead and make you feel bad about your decision. Ignore the noise. Your culture, identity, and Blackness go with you no matter where you are.

What matters isn't where you go, it's how you navigate that space. And you? You belong wherever you are.

THE COLLEGE APPLICATION PROCESS – RECAP
Most universities accept applications through the Common App at the time of this writing. It's a one-stop solution for uploading essays, answering questions, and submitting transcripts. Use it.

FAFSA – REQUIRED FOR EVERYONE
Regardless of whether you're financially well-off, you must complete the FAFSA to determine your aid eligibility.

- Pell Grants = Free Money. If you qualify, you don't have to pay it back.

- If your parents make too much money, aid might be minimal. That's why it's crucial to apply for scholarships.
- Weigh your financial options. College is an investment. Make the most intelligent financial choice for YOU.

SCHOLARSHIPS EXIST—GO FIND THEM

Many high schools pay for access to private scholarship databases. Check with your academic counselor; this is free money that doesn't need to be repaid. Remember that every dollar you earn in scholarships = one less dollar in student loans.

FINAL WORDS: MAKE IT COUNT

This playbook was never about perfection. It's about awareness, showing up, asking for help, staying grounded in who you are, and moving with intention. Don't wait until you're overwhelmed to ask for help. Don't shrink to fit into spaces not made for you. Don't play small to make others comfortable.

Always remember…

- Never compromise your Blackness.
- You worked hard to get here; maximize the opportunity.
- Your journey is YOURS. Adjust as needed, but never doubt yourself.
- Use your resources, trust your instincts, and seize every opportunity.

At a PWI, you might feel overlooked, misunderstood,

or even underestimated. But let that fuel you. Use every tool. Build your network. Protect your peace. You are more than ready. More than capable. And more than qualified. Use what's in this book. Use your story. Use your strength. Be resilient. And above all, move smart.

The next few years will shape your future. Make them count.

You got this!!

Appendix A: Resource Directory

Appendix A - This section includes essential digital tools, mobile apps, and professional organizations across common majors. These resources are here to help you stay organized, stay safe, and stay connected.

Digital Tools & Apps

Note-taking & Organization

- Notion (all-in-one workspace)
- Evernote (note organization)
- OneNote (digital notebook)
- Google Keep (quick notes and reminders)

Study Aids

- Quizlet (flashcards and study sets)
- Forest (productivity and focus timer)
- Anki (advanced flashcard system)
- Khan Academy (free educational videos)

Financial Management

- Mint (budgeting and expense tracking)
- YNAB (You Need A Budget)
- Splitwise (expense sharing with roommates)
- CashApp/Venmo (peer-to-peer payments)

Campus Safety

- Circle of 6 (quickly contact trusted friends)

APPENDIX A: RESOURCE DIRECTORY

- LiveSafe (campus security connection)
- bSafe (location sharing and emergency alerts)
- Rave Guardian (campus safety app)

Career & Networking

- LinkedIn (professional networking)
- Handshake (campus recruiting platform)
- Slack (professional communication)
- Indeed/Glassdoor (job searching)

PROFESSIONAL ORGANIZATIONS BY MAJOR

Business & Administration

- **National Black MBA Association (NBMBAA):** This organization is dedicated to enhancing educational and economic empowerment for African Americans. It offers networking opportunities, career fairs, and professional development programs.

- **American Society for Public Administration (ASPA):** While not exclusively for Black professionals, ASPA promotes public and non-profit administration advancements, providing valuable resources and networking opportunities.

- **National Association of Health Services Executives (NAHSE):** A non-profit association of Black health care executives founded for the purpose of promoting the advancement and development of

Appendix A: Resource Directory

Black health care leaders, and elevating the quality of health care services rendered to minority and underserved communities.

Social Sciences & Psychology

- **National Economic Association (NEA)**: Focused on producing and distributing professional knowledge related to economic issues that are of exceptional interest to promoting the economic growth of Black people.

- **Association of Black Psychologists (ABPsi)**: This organization seeks to address the psychological needs of Black people by promoting and advancing the profession of African Psychology.

Communications & Journalism

- **National Association of Black Journalists (NABJ)**: An organization of Black journalists, students, and media professionals that provides quality programs and services to and advocates on behalf of Black journalists worldwide.

Engineering & Computer Science

- **National Society of Black Engineers (NSBE)**: With a mission to increase the number of culturally responsible Black engineers who excel academically, succeed professionally, and positively impact the community, NSBE offers extensive resources, networking, and support.

Appendix A: Resource Directory

- **ColorStack**: A nonprofit organization that provides support and community for Black and Latinx computer science students, aiming to increase their representation in the tech industry.

Education

- **National Alliance of Black School Educators (NABSE)**: Dedicated to improving the educational accomplishments of African American youth through the development and deployment of instructional and motivational methods that increase levels of inspiration, attendance, and overall achievement.

Law & Legal Studies

- **National Bar Association (NBA)**: The nation's oldest and largest national network of predominantly African-American attorneys and judges, offering professional development, networking, and advocacy.

Healthcare & Medicine

- **National Pharmaceutical Association (NPhA)**: Dedicated to representing the views and ideals of minority pharmacists on critical issues affecting healthcare and pharmacy, focusing on improving the quality of healthcare in underserved communities.

- **National Association of Black Physical Therapists **(NABPT)**: Founded to address the unique challenges faced by minorities in the field of physical therapy, NABPT aims to increase diversity within PT educational programs and the profession as a whole. The organization provides visibility, networking, community service, advocacy, career development, and mentorship opportunities for Black physical therapists and physical therapist assistants.

- **National Dental Association (NDA)**: Established in 1913, the NDA is a professional association of minority dentists. It aims to promote oral health equity among people of color by providing education, support, and programs for Black dentists throughout their careers.

- **Association of Black Women Dentists**: Founded on May 11, 2018, this national organization focuses on supporting Black women in the dental profession, providing networking opportunities, mentorship, and advocacy.

- **Black Nurses Rock**: Established in 2015, this organization represents over 174,000 African American nurses and students globally. It focuses on fostering a community of collaboration, professional development, and support among Black nurses.

- **National Black Nurses Association (NBNA)**: Founded in 1971, the NBNA represents African American nurses across the U.S., Canada, Eastern Caribbean, and Africa. Its mission is to provide a forum for collective action by African American nurses to advocate for and implement strategies ensuring access to the highest quality of healthcare for persons of color.

- **Underrepresented Minorities in Interventional Radiology (URM in IR)**: A section within the Society of Interventional Radiology, URM in IR focuses on increasing the presence of underrepresented minorities in the field at all career levels, improving awareness of interventional radiology medical care to minorities, promoting diversity of thought on committees, and working to eradicate healthcare disparities affecting minorities.

Creative & Design Fields

- **National Organization of Minority Architects (NOMA)**: Aims to champion diversity within the design professions by promoting the excellence, community engagement, and professional development of its members.

- **National Conference of Artists (NCA)**: The oldest African American visual arts organization in the United States, dedicated to preserving, promoting, and developing the African American cultural and artistic traditions.

Sports & Physical Education

- **National Association of Black Sports Professionals (NABSP)**: NABSP focuses on increasing

Appendix A: Resource Directory

the representation and advancement of Black professionals in sports-related fields, including athletic training and coaching. The organization offers networking opportunities, professional development, and advocacy for its members.

- **National Society of Black Sports Professionals (NSBSP)**: NSBSP aims to empower Black professionals in the sports industry, including athletic trainers and coaches, by providing networking events, professional development programs, and mentorship opportunities. The organization focuses on fostering a supportive community to promote career advancement and representation in sports.

- **Black Coaches and Administrators (BCA)**: BCA is an organization dedicated to the advancement of Black coaches, administrators, and sports professionals. It provides resources, mentorship, and advocacy to support career development and address issues related to diversity and inclusion in coaching and sports administration.

Culinary Arts

- **BCAGlobal (formerly Black Culinarian Alliance)**: Established in 1998, BCAGlobal aims to empower BIPOC individuals in the food system, including the food service industry. Their mission encompasses mindfulness, sustainability, social justice, and food sovereignty, helping to forge meaningful connections within the culinary community.

Appendix A: Resource Directory

- **Black Chef's Network**: Founded and incorporated in 2015, this organization was created for African-American and minority culinary professionals. It offers a platform for networking, professional development, and collaboration among Black chefs.

- **National Black Chef's Association**: This association engages individuals in the catering service, including pastry chefs and cooks, fostering a community within the food industry.

- **Association of African American Chefs**: A community of chefs of African descent, this group celebrates the unique contributions and talents of Black chefs in the culinary arts.

Appendix B: Checklists & Worksheets

Appendix B - This section is your toolkit, featuring packing lists, personal safety plans, budgeting sheets, and academic planners. These plug-and-play tools help you prepare, track, and thrive during each college phase.

First Year Preparation Checklist

Before Arrival

- [ ] Complete housing paperwork
- [ ] Connect with roommate(s)
- [ ] Register for orientation
- [ ] Review course requirements
- [ ] Finalize financial aid
- [ ] Set up bank account near campus
- [ ] Get health insurance documentation
- [ ] Prepare packing list (see below)

Packing Essentials

- [ ] Important documents (ID, insurance cards, financial aid info)
- [ ] Bedding and room decor
- [ ] Toiletries and personal care items
- [ ] School supplies
- [ ] Electronics and chargers
- [ ] Appropriate clothing for all seasons
- [ ] Medications and first aid supplies
- [ ] Small tool kit and emergency supplies

First Week

- [ ] Attend orientation events
- [ ] Locate important campus buildings
- [ ] Meet academic advisor
- [ ] Finalize class schedule
- [ ] Purchase/rent textbooks
- [ ] Explore dining options
- [ ] Locate cultural centers and resources
- [ ] Learn campus safety procedures

First Semester Milestones

- [ ] Join at least one student organization
- [ ] Attend professor office hours at least once
- [ ] Create a study schedule
- [ ] Find preferred study locations
- [ ] Connect with academic support services
- [ ] Attend a campus cultural event
- [ ] Begin building your professional network
- [ ] Schedule advising appointment for next semester

Appendix B: Checklists & Worksheets

Personal Safety Plan Template

Emergency Contacts

- Campus Police: _____
- Local Police: _____
- Campus Health Center: _____
- Counseling Services: _____
- Residential Advisor: _____
- Trusted Friend 1: _____
- Trusted Friend 2: _____
- Family Contact: _____

Safe Transportation Options

- Campus Shuttle Hours: _____
- Campus Escort Service: _____
- Rideshare Apps: _____
- Local Taxi: _____
- Public Transportation: _____

Safety Strategies

- Location sharing apps with trusted friends
- Regular check-ins when out late
- Safe meeting spots on campus
- Code words with friends for uncomfortable situations
- Campus areas to avoid after dark
- Party safety plan (arrival together, departure together)

If You Feel Unsafe...

- Move to a well-lit, populated area
- Contact campus security
- Text your safety circle
- Use campus emergency phones if available
- Trust your instincts and remove yourself from situations that feel wrong

Appendix B: Checklists & Worksheets

College Budget Worksheet

Income Sources

Category	Monthly Amount
Financial Aid/Scholarships	$_____
Family Contribution	$_____
Work-Study/Job	$_____
Side Hustles	$_____
Other	$_____
TOTAL INCOME	**$_____**

Fixed Expenses

Category	Monthly Amount
Tuition/Fees Payment	$_____
Housing	$_____
Meal Plan/Groceries	$_____
Phone	$_____
Insurance	$_____
Subscriptions	$_____
Loan Payments	$_____
TOTAL FIXED EXPENSES	**$_____**

Variable Expenses

Category	Monthly Amount
Books/Supplies	$_____
Transportation	$_____
Entertainment	$_____
Eating Out	$_____
Personal Care	$_____
Clothing	$_____
Miscellaneous	$_____
TOTAL VARIABLE EXPENSES	**$_____**

Savings

Category	Monthly Amount
Emergency Fund	$_____
Future Goals	$_____
TOTAL SAVINGS	**$_____**

Summary

- **Total Income: $_____**
- **Total Expenses: $_____**
- **Net Balance: $_____**

Appendix B: Checklists & Worksheets

Four-Year Academic Planning Sheet

FIRST YEAR

Fall Semester	Credits	Spring Semester	Credits
1. _____	1. _____		
2. _____	2. _____		
3. _____	3. _____		
4. _____	4. _____		
5. _____	5. _____	Total Credits: I ___	Total Credits: I ___

Summer Plans: _____

SECOND YEAR

Fall Semester	Credits	Spring Semester	Credits
1. _____	1. _____		
2. _____	2. _____		
3. _____	3. _____		
4. _____	4. _____		
5. _____	5. _____	Total Credits: I ___	Total Credits: I ___

Summer Plans: _____

THIRD YEAR

Fall Semester	Credits	Spring Semester	Credits
1. _____	1. _____		
2. _____	2. _____		
3. _____	3. _____		
4. _____	4. _____		
5. _____	5. _____	Total Credits: I ___	Total Credits: I ___

Summer Plans: _____

FOURTH YEAR

Fall Semester	Credits	Spring Semester	Credits
1. _____	1. _____		
2. _____	2. _____		
3. _____	3. _____		
4. _____	4. _____		
5. _____	5. _____	Total Credits: I ___	Total Credits: I ___

Graduation Requirements Tracker

- Required Credits: ___ / ___ completed
- Major Requirements: ___ / ___ completed
- General Education: ___ / ___ completed
- Electives: ___ / ___ completed
- GPA: ___

Appendix C: Additional Resources

Appendix C - A curated list of forums, scholarship programs, and online communities built to support Black students. If you're looking to expand your knowledge, find funding, or connect with others, this is where to start.

Online Communities & Forums

- **Black Student Collective** - Online forum connecting Black students across PWIs

- **HBCU Hub** - Resource sharing platform even for non-HBCU students

- **Black Career Network** - Professional development community

- **Black Student Alliance Network** - National coalition of campus BSUs

- **The Blackprint** - News and information hub for Black college students

- **NSBE Talk** - Online discussion board by National Society of Black Engineers

Scholarship Resources for Black Students

- **United Negro College Fund (UNCF)** - Provides scholarships exclusively for Black students

- **Thurgood Marshall College Fund** - Supports stu-

Appendix C: Additional Resources

dents at public HBCUs

- **Jackie Robinson Foundation** - Four-year scholarship program

- **Ron Brown Scholar Program** - For community-minded African American students

- **NAACP Scholarships** - Various programs for Black students

- **National Black MBA Association Scholarships** - For business students

- **The Gates Scholarship** - For exceptional minority students with financial need

- **Black Excellence Scholarship Database** - Comprehensive listing of opportunities

- **Jesse Brown Scholarship** - For disabled veterans and their family members

- **Blacks at Microsoft Scholarship** - For students pursuing tech careers

- **High School Guidance Counselor Resources** - Many high school guidance offices pay for access to comprehensive scholarship databases that students can use for free - be sure to check with your counselor before graduation

Remember...
You belong here and come from royalty.
Head up. Shoulders back.
You got this!

Author Bio

J. McCarthy, PhD, MBA (aka Dr. Jay) is a consultant, educator, and lifelong mentor dedicated to empowering young minds through education, leadership, and sports. With a PhD in Advanced Studies in Human Behavior, an MBA, and a BS in eMarketing, he has built a career spanning business analytics, instructional technology, and nonprofit leadership.

Beyond his professional expertise, Dr. Jay is deeply committed to youth advocacy and mentorship. He founded and operated his youth sports club, where he coached and guided young athletes, using sports as a vehicle for personal development and life skills.

Through his mentorship programs, he has helped countless young men and women navigate education, careers, and life's challenges with confidence.

An Ohio native (Go Bucks!), Dr. Jay now resides in the Dallas-Fort Worth area with his wife, Marla, and their seven children, six boys and one baby girl, plus an extended family of mentees. He brings a personal, heartfelt perspective to his writing, sharing the lessons he's learned as both a mentor and a parent.

A thought leader in college readiness, workplace dynamics, and personal growth, Dr. Jay writes with a blend of scholarly insight and real-world wisdom. His books offer practical advice and encouragement, ensuring readers walk away empowered and prepared for the next stage of life.

ALSO AVAILABLE FROM
THE REAL LIFE SERIES PUBLISHING CO.

Managing the Imbalance: From Burnout to Breakthrough
Reclaiming Your Time, Energy, and What Matters Most
by J. McCarthy, PhD, MBA
ISBN: 979-8-9989754-0-0

Managing the Imbalance: Behind the Whistle
Coaching Others Without Compromising Yourself
by J. McCarthy, PhD, MBA
ISBN: 979-8-9989754-7-9

www.ingramcontent.com/pod-product-compliance
Lightning Source LLC
Chambersburg PA
CBHW020546030426
42337CB00013B/985